# DIAL 911!

By CHARLES GHIGNA

Illustrations by GLENN THOMAS

Music by MARK OBLINGER

CANTATA
LEARNING

WWW.CANTATALEARNING.COM

# CANTATA
# LEARNING

Published by Cantata Learning
1710 Roe Crest Drive
North Mankato, MN 56003
www.cantatalearning.com

**Library of Congress Cataloging-in-Publication Data**
Title: Dial 911! / by Charles Ghigna ; Illustrations by Glenn Thomas ; music
by Mark Oblinger.
Description: North Mankato, MN : Cantata Learning, [2018] | Series: Fire
safety | Audience: Age 3-8. | Audience: K to grade 3.
Identifiers: LCCN 2017007522 (print) | LCCN 2017016716 (ebook) | ISBN
9781684100200 | ISBN 9781684100729 (pbk. : alk. paper) | ISBN
9781684100194 (hardcover : alk. paper)
Subjects: LCSH: Fires--Safety measures--Juvenile literature. | Fire
prevention--Juvenile literature. | Telephone--Emergency reporting
systems--Juvenile literature.
Classification: LCC TH9148 (ebook) | LCC TH9148 .G45 2018 (print) | DDC
613.6--dc23
LC record available at https://lccn.loc.gov/2017007522

Book design, Tim Palin Creative
Editorial direction, Flat Sole Studio
Executive musical production and direction, Elizabeth Draper
Music arranged and produced by Mark Oblinger

Printed in the United States of America in North Mankato, Minnesota.
072017                    0367CGF17

ACCESS THE MUSIC!

SCAN CODE WITH MOBILE APP

CANTATALEARNING.COM

# TIPS TO SUPPORT LITERACY AT HOME

## WHY READING AND SINGING WITH YOUR CHILD IS SO IMPORTANT

Daily reading with your child leads to increased academic achievement. Music and songs, specifically rhyming songs, are a fun and easy way to build early literacy and language development. Music skills correlate significantly with both phonological awareness and reading development. Singing helps build vocabulary and speech development. And reading and appreciating music together is a wonderful way to strengthen your relationship.

### *READ AND SING EVERY DAY!*

## TIPS FOR USING CANTATA LEARNING BOOKS AND SONGS DURING YOUR DAILY STORY TIME

1. As you sing and read, point out the different words on the page that rhyme. Suggest other words that rhyme.

2. Memorize simple rhymes such as Itsy Bitsy Spider and sing them together. This encourages comprehension skills and early literacy skills.

3. Use the questions in the back of each book to guide your singing and storytelling.

4. Read the included sheet music with your child while you listen to the song. How do the music notes correlate to the words of the song?

5. Sing along on the go and at home. Access music by scanning the QR code on each Cantata book. You can also stream or download the music for free to your computer, smartphone, or mobile device.

Devoting time to daily reading shows that you are available for your child. Together, you are building language, literacy, and listening skills.

Have fun reading and singing!

Fire safety starts with you! If there is a fire in your home, what should you do? Get out and call for help. Dial 9-1-1! Firefighters will be on the way to **save the day**.

Now turn the page to practice this important fire safety skill. Remember to sing along!

If you see fire, get away!

Then dial this number to save the day:

9-1-1!

9-1-1!

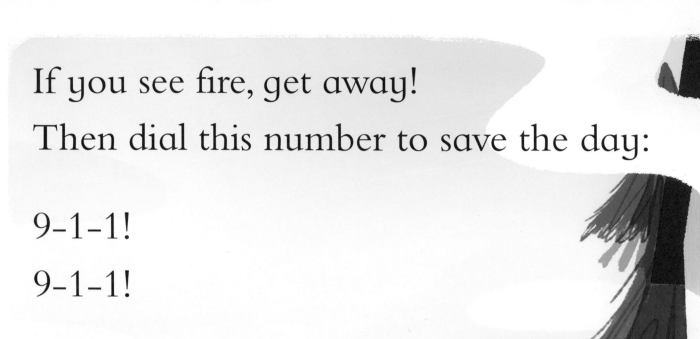

Help is coming on the run.
If you need help, call 9-1-1.

Fire trucks, here they come!
Sirens howling, hear them hum!

Fire trucks roll down the street.
Firefighters don't miss a beat.

Firefighters know what to do.
Stand back. See how they help you.

They grab a ladder and a hose.
Flames jump up. Water flows.

If you see fire, get away!
Then dial this number to save the day:

9-1-1!

9-1-1!

Help is coming on the run!

If you need help, call 9-1-1.

Cheer and shout!
The fire is out!

14

Cheer and shout!
The fire is out!

Ladders slide back in their slots.
Pet the **fire dog** and his spots!

Hoses are rolled and stored away.

**Gear** is ready for another day.

Firefighters do their job so well.
Reach up high to ring the bell!

You called and help came on the run.
Firefighters answer 9-1-1!

If you see fire, get away!
Then dial this number to save the day:

9-1-1!

9-1-1!

Help is coming on the run!

If you need help, call 9-1-1.

If you need help, call 9-1-1.

If you need help, call 9-1-1.

# SONG LYRICS
## Dial 911!

If you see fire, get away!
Then dial this number to save the day:
9-1-1!
9-1-1!
Help is coming on the run.
If you need help, call 9-1-1.

Fire trucks, here they come!
Sirens howling, hear them hum!
Fire trucks roll down the street.
Firefighters don't miss a beat.

Firefighters know what to do.
Stand back. See how they help you.
They grab a ladder and a hose.
Flames jump up. Water flows.

If you see fire, get away!
Then dial this number to save the day:
9-1-1!
9-1-1!
Help is coming on the run!
If you need help, call 9-1-1.

Cheer and shout!
The fire is out!
Cheer and shout!
The fire is out!

Ladders slide back in their slots.
Pet the fire dog and his spots!
Hoses are rolled and stored away.
Gear is ready for another day.

Firefighters do their job so well.
Reach up high to ring the bell!
You called and help came on the run.
Firefighters answer 9-1-1!

If you see fire, get away!
Then dial this number to save the day:
9-1-1!
9-1-1!
Help is coming on the run!
If you need help, call 9-1-1.
If you need help, call 9-1-1.
If you need help, call 9-1-1.

# Dial 911!

**Rock and Roll**
Mark Oblinger

**Chorus**

If you see fi - re, get a - way! Then dial this num - ber to save the day: 9 - 1 - 1! 9 - 1 - 1!

Help is com - ing on the run. If you need help, call 9 - 1 - 1.

**Verse**

1. Fi - re trucks, here they come! Si - rens howl - ing, hear them hum! Fi - re trucks roll down the street. Fi - re - fight - ers don't miss a beat.

**Interlude**

**Verse 2**
Firefighters know what to do.
Stand back. See how they help you.
They grab a ladder and a hose.
Flames jump up. Water flows.

**Interlude**

**Chorus**

**Bridge**

Cheer and shout! The fi - re is out! Cheer and shout! The fi - re is out!

**Interlude**

**Verse 3**
Ladders slide back in their slots.
Pet the fire dog and his spots!
Hoses are rolled and stored away.
Gear is ready for another day.

**Interlude**

**Verse 4**
Firefighters do their job so well.
Reach up high to ring the bell!
You called and help came on the run.
Firefighters answer 9-1-1!

**Interlude**

**Outro**

If you see fi - re, get a - way! Then dial this num - ber to save the day: 9 - 1 - 1! 9 - 1 - 1!

(3x)

Help is com - ing on the run. If you need help, call 9 - 1 - 1.

# GLOSSARY

**fire dog**—a dog who lives at the fire station; the firefighters' pet

**gear**—clothes and equipment needed to do a job

**save the day**—to perform a rescue or solve a hard problem

# GUIDED READING ACTIVITIES

1.  Show 9-1-1 with your hands. Flash nine fingers. Then flash one finger and one finger again. Listen to the song again. Every time you hear 9-1-1, show it with your hands.

2.  Look back at pages 12 and 13. Then make a poster showing people what to do in case of an emergency. Hang it in your house to remind your family to call 9-1-1.

3.  Interview adults in your life. Ask them if they have ever called 9-1-1. What happened?

TO LEARN MORE

Guard, Anara. *What If You Need to Call 911?* North Mankato, MN: Capstone, 2012.

Lyons, Shelly. *Safety in My Neighborhood.* North Mankato, MN: Capstone, 2013.

Ulz, Ivan. *Fire Truck!* Halycon, CA: Temple Street Press, 2013.

Yolen, Jane. *How Do Dinosaurs Stay Safe?* New York: The Blue Sky Press, 2015.